Wildflowers of Arizona & New Mexico

George Miller

Adventure Quick Guides

YOUR WAY TO EASILY IDENTIFY WILDFLOWERS

Adventure Quick Guides

With three named deserts, as well as plateaus, grasslands, forests, and snow-covered mountains, Arizona and New Mexico harbor a vast diversity of wildflower communities. The photos and succinct descriptions in this Quick Guide describe 248 wildflowers and cacti you'll find in the Southwest, from common and showy plants to rare and stunning specimens. To aid identification, a photograph illustrates each species and a short description lists the plant's size and unique flower and leaf characteristics. Sized to easily fit into a pocket or a pack, it will introduce you to the jewel-like flowers that fill meadows and line trails and roadsides. For more detailed descriptions and photos, visit the author's website www.wildflowersNM.com.

GEORGE OXFORD MILLER

Long-time botanist and nature photographer George Miller is a lifelong resident of the West. He has lived in New Mexico, Arizona, and Texas, and currently is president of the Albuquerque chapter of the Native Plant Society of New Mexico. He received a master's degree in zoology and botany, from The University of Texas, Austin, and has written six guidebooks to the Southwest, including the best-seller *Landscaping with Native Plants of the Southwest*, five other Wildflower Quick Guides, and a "Plant of the Month" column in *New Mexico Magazine*. His wildflower website, www.wildflowersNM.com, describes nearly 600 species with photos and identification tips.

Cover and book design by Lora Westberg
Edited by Brett Ortler

Cover image: Purple geranium *(Geranium caespitosum)* by George Miller

All images by George Miller.

10 9 8 7 6 5 4 3 2 1

Wildflowers of Arizona & New Mexico

Published by Adventure Publications, an imprint of AdventureKEEN
330 Garfield Street South, Cambridge, Minnesota 55008
(800) 678-7006
www.adventurepublications.net

Printed in China
ISBN 978-1-59193-817-0 (pbk.)

How to Use This Guide

KEY

- Wildflowers are sorted into four groups by color and organized within groups from smaller to larger blooms.
- Leaf attachment icons are shown next to each wildflower.
- Descriptions include important facts such as cluster shape, number of petals, or center color to help you quickly identify the species. Size information is sometimes included as well.

LEAF ATTACHMENT

Wildflower leaves attach to stems in different ways. The leaf icons next to the flowers show alternate, opposite, whorled, perfoliate, clasping, and basal attachments. Some wildflower plants have two or more types of leaf attachments.

ALTERNATE leaves attach in an alternating pattern.

OPPOSITE leaves attach directly opposite each other.

BASAL leaves originate at the base of the plant and are usually grouped in pairs or in a rosette.

PERFOLIATE leaves are stalkless and have a leaf base that completely surrounds the main stem.

CLASPING leaves have no stalk, and the base partly surrounds the main stem.

WHORLED leaves have three or more leaves that attach around the stem at the same point.

CLUSTERED leaves originate from the same point on the stem.

SPINES are leaves that take the form of sharp spines.

PARTS OF A FLOWER

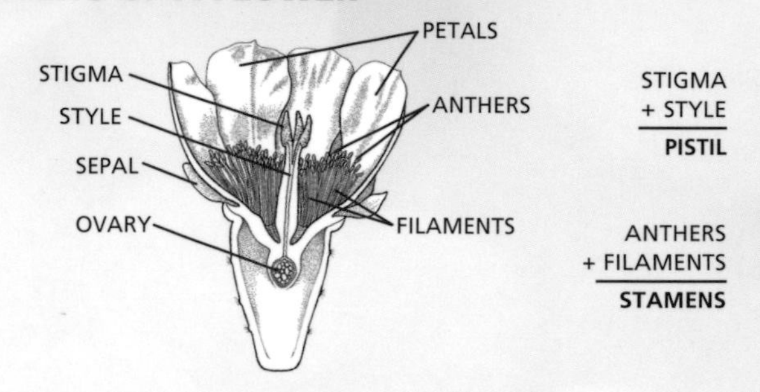

DESERTS, MOUNTAINS, PLATEAUS, AND GRASSLANDS

Arizona and New Mexico include some of the most spectacular and dynamic landscapes in the American West. Heading north from the arid U.S.-Mexico border, the landscape steadily gains elevation and moisture levels rise. Two mighty rivers, the Rio Grande and the Colorado, also cross through the region, and numerous tributaries provide a perennial water source for plants and wildlife. The Mojave, Sonora, and Chihuahua deserts extend into the heart of the region, supporting some of the most diverse—and fragile—communities in North America.

In the northern parts of both states, tectonic uplifting of the Colorado Plateau formed vast expanses of shrubby brush and grasslands. As the plateau inched upward to the present 7,000-plus-foot elevation, the unrelenting forces of erosion carved tangled canyonlands, sculptured multicolored badlands, and verdant river valleys. This great diversity of landforms has fostered a unique mosaic of plant communities. Some blend into each other with gradual changes, while the stark contrast between others is stunning. Rivers and springs create ribbons of green through sunbaked landscapes, and mountains with snow-capped peaks and lush canyons punctuate xeric tablelands of cacti and brush. Mountain islands surrounded by deserts form refuges for birds, mammals, and other animal life. Such isolated environments have allowed plants to adapt into species that occur nowhere else on Earth.

From luxuriant meadows waist-high with wildflowers to a lone flower found blooming like a lost jewel on a sunbaked hillside, Arizona and New Mexico's wildflowers offer a wondrous variety of wildflowers to behold.

Cymopterus glomeratus

Fendler's Springparsley

Stems to 7 inches tall; umbrella-like cluster of tiny flowers; parsley-like leaves; early spring

Cymopterus lemmonii

Mountain Parsley

Stems to 2 feet; flat clusters of tiny flowers; parsley-like basal leaves, smaller stem leaves

Ericameria nauseosa

Chamisa, Rabbitbrush

Shrub 3–6 feet; dense clusters of tiny disk flowers cover plant, no rays; narrow or absent leaves

Gutierrezia sarothrae

Broom Snakeweed

Densely branching, 1–2-feet; small flower heads with 3–8 rays; yellow disk; narrow leaves

Hymenopappus filifolius

Fine-leaf Woolly-White

Stems 2–5 feet; many flower heads with disk flowers only; leaves with narrow, linear segments

Solidago altissima

Tall Goldenrod

Stems 2–6 feet; flowers in plume-like clusters, tiny rays; lance-shaped, scratchy leaves

Eriogonum umbellatum

Sulphur Flower Buckwheat

Leafless stems to 12 inches tall; spherical clusters of yellow flowers; oval mat-forming leaves

Physaria fendleri

Fendler's Bladderpod

Stems 4–14 inches; flowers have 4 petals; fruit a hollow sphere; oval to lance-shaped leaves

Draba helleriana

Twisted-pod Draba

Hairy stems to 16 inches; rounded flower clusters; flat, twisted seed-pod; oblong leaves

Tribulus terrestris

Goathead

Mat-forming stems to 3 feet wide; 5 yellow petals; fruit a thorny nutlet; elliptical leaflets

Chamaesaracha coronopus

Greenleaf Five Eyes

Stems 4–20 inches tall; yellow-green flower with 5-points; narrow, hairy, wavy or lobed leaves

Physalis hederifolia

Ivyleaf Groundcherry

Stems bushy to 32 inches; drooping, hat-shaped flower with dark center; toothed leaves

Agave parryi

Parry's Agave

Flower in flat, dense clusters on stalks 9–18 feet tall; sword-like leaves have spines on edges, tips

Agoseris aurantiaca

Burnt-orange Dandelion

Stems 4–24 inches; narrow, toothed rays, no disk flowers; elliptical or lobed leaves; milky sap

Malacothrix fendleri

Fendler's Desert Dandelion

Stems to 1 foot; ray florets are square-tipped with 5 points; linear, toothed leaves; milky sap

Pectis angustifolia

Limoncillo

Low stems to 8 inches tall; flower heads with 8 rays; yellow disk; linear, lemon-scented leaves

Thymophylla pentachaeta

Fiveneedle Dogweed

Stems 4–8 inches; long flower stalks; dime-sized flower head; leaves have stiff, thread-like lobes

Heterotheca subaxillaris

Camphor Weed

Stems 1–3 feet; flower with 15–35+ yellow rays; yellow disk; oval to lance-shaped leaves

Hymenoxys odorata

Bitterweed

Clumps 2 feet wide; many flower heads, notched rays, yellow disk; filament-like leaves

Cevallia sinuata

Stinging Cevallia

Stems 1–3 feet, foliage with stinging hairs; flowers in dense cluster; lance-shaped, lobed leaves

Asclepias tuberosa

Butterfly Milkweed

Hairy stems to 3 feet; yellow to orange flowers; hairy, narrow, lance-shaped leaves; clear sap

Berberis repens

Creeping Barberry

Groundcover; clusters of small, yellow flowers; leaflets lined with prickles; blue berries

Corydalis aurea

Golden Corydalis

Stems 8–14 inches; spike of flowers, petals form curved tube with spur; parsley-like leaflets

Mimulus guttatus

Yellow Monkeyflower

Stems 2–3 feet; lower flower lobe bearded with red spots; rounded leaves; in wet areas

Giant Helleborine Orchid

Leafy stems 1–3 feet; orangish-brown flowers with reddish streaks; clasping leaves; streamsides

Hog Potato

Stems 6–12 inches; stem and flower dotted with red glands; leaflets oval along midrib

Golden Pea

Stems 1–2 feet; spike dense with pea-like flowers; leaves have 3 leaflets; mountains

Curlycup Gumweed

Stems 1–3 feet; flower heads resinous, sticky; rays usually absent; lance-shaped, toothed leaves

Indian Tea

Flower stalks 12–32 inches tall; disk flowers only, no rays; leaves have thread-like lobes

Ragleaf Bahia

Stems to 32 inches; ray florets with notched tips; yellow disk; leaf lobes deeply divided

Hairy Golden Aster

Hairy stems to 20 inches tall; flower heads with 7–21 rays; short, hairy, widely spaced leaves

Warty Caltrop

Mat-forming stems 20–40 inches long; 5 orange petals with a reddish tint; elliptical leaflets

Oxalis dillenii

Yellow Wood Sorrel

Stems 4–10 inches; 5 solid-yellow petals with notched tips; leaves have 3 heart-shaped leaflets

Senna bauhinioides

Twin-leaf Senna

Stems 4–16 inches; oval petals with narrow base; hairy leaves with twin oval leaflets

Larrea tridentata

Creosote Bush

Rounded desert shrub; 5 propeller-like twisted petals; fuzzy white fruit; aromatic leaves

Potentilla hippiana

Silverweed Cinquefoil

Silky stems to 20 inches; clusters of flowers; showy stamens; toothed leaflets along midrib

Ranunculus inamoenus

Fanleaf Buttercup

Stems 2–13 inches; 5–10 petals, showy stamens; roundish undivided or lobed leaves

Verbascum thapsus

Woolly Mullein

Bloom stalks to 6 feet; spikes of yellow flowers, 5 petals; large, fuzzy leaves; roadside invasive

Cirsium parryi

Parry's Thistle

Stems 2–6 feet; spiny, cobwebby flower heads; spine-tipped, toothed leaves; mountains

Packera neomexicana

New Mexico Groundsel

Stems 8–20 inches; many flower heads, 8–13 rays, yellow disk; lance- to egg-shaped leaves

Senecio flaccidus

Threadleaf Groundsel

Stems 1–4 feet; clusters of flowers; 8 or 13 narrow rays; thread-like, gray-woolly leaflets

Lithospermum incisum

Fringed Puccoon

Stems 6–12 inches; trumpet-shaped flowers; lobes crinkly-edged; linear to oblong leaves

Sphaeralcea hastulata

Spear Globemallow

Stems 6–12 inches; orange-red flowers; lance-shaped hairy leaves with 2 pointed basal lobes

Hypericum scouleri

Western St. John's Wort

Stems 1–2 feet; clustered flowers; black dots line petals; oval, black-dotted leaves; moist forests

Erysimum capitatum

Wallflower

Stems to 30 inches; rounded clusters of orange or yellow flowers; erect long seedpods around stem

Hymenoxys richardsonii

Pingue Rubberweed

Stems to 1 foot; 7–20 rays notched with 3 points; yellow disk; filament-like, lobed leaves

Tetraneuris argentea

Perky Sue

Stems to 10 inches with 1 flower each; 8–14 notched rays, yellow disk; hairy, slender leaves

Berlandiera lyrata

Chocolate Flower

Stems 1–2 feet; rays have notched tips, red veins underneath; maroon disk; lobed leaves

Viguiera dentata

Plateau Golden-Eye

Stems 3–6 feet; 10–14 rays with notched tip; yellow disk; leaves oval to lance-shaped, serrated

Heliomeris multiflora

Showy Goldeneye

Stems to 4 feet with many flower heads; golden rays, yellow disk; elliptic to lance-shaped leaves

Encelia farinosa

Brittlebush

Bushy; flowers on long, hairless stems; disk brown or yellow; woolly, slivery leaves; AZ

Taraxacum officinale

Dandelion

Hollow stems 1–10 inches; flower head has 100+ rays, no disk; arrow-shaped leaf lobes

Xanthisma spinulosum

Spiny Golden Aster

Stems 6–18 inches; flower heads with 14–60 narrow rays; disk yellow; bristly leaf lobes

Zinnia grandiflora

Plains Zinnia

Clumps to 8 inches tall; 3–6 oval, bright yellow rays, orange disk; thin, linear leaves

Abutilon palmeri

Indian Mallow

Shrubby; yellow-orange petals, showy stamens; heart-shaped, velvety leaves; AZ

Calochortus aureus

Yellow Mariposa Lily

1–4 flowers from bulb; petals golden with maroon crescent near base; leaves narrow blades

Baileya multiradiata

Desert Marigold

Stems 12–18 inches; head packed with rays with 3 notches; yellow disk; lobed, woolly leaves

Bahia absinthifolia

Sageleaf Bahia

Stems 4–16 inches; yellow ray florets, yellow-orange disk; hairy, gray-blue, 3-lobed leaves

Helianthus petiolaris

Plains Sunflower

Stems 1–3 feet; showy rays; disk brown, center often whitish; triangular to lance-shaped leaves

Mentzelia multiflora

Adonis Blazing Star

Stems to 32 inches; yellow to creamy flowers, showy stamens; lobed, clasping, Velcro-like leaves

Helianthus annuus

Annual Sunflower

Single stems 2– 8 feet, 20+ flowers; yellow rays, reddish-brown disk; triangular leaves

Verbesina encelioides

Cowpen Daisy

Stems 1–3 feet; rays with 3 deep notches; yellow disk; broad, triangular, toothed, rough leaves

Scabrethia scabra

Badlands Mule-ears

Clumps to 2 feet tall; rays and disk are yellow; long, narrow, rough leaves with distinct midvein

Ratibida columnifera

Prairie Coneflower

Stems 1– 4 feet; yellow, maroon, or blended rays; cylindrical, brown disk; lobed leaves

Orange Sneezeweed

Stems 2–3+ feet; rays fold lengthwise and droop; yellow-orange disk; linear to lance-shaped leaves

Cutleaf Coneflower

Stems 2–7 feet; domed head has drooping rays; yellow disk; leaves deeply lobed along midrib

Desert Hibiscus

Shrubby 1–3 feet; petals creamy yellow with purple basal spot, showy stamens; 3-lobed leaves

California Poppy

Flowers with 4 gold-to-orange petals blanket hillsides; leaves have fern-like lobes; yellow sap

Hooker's Evening Primrose

Stems to 8 feet; dense clusters of yellow flowers; erect, hairy buds; elliptical to lance-shaped leaves

Hartweg's Sundrops

Leafy mounding stems to 18 inches; 4 crinkly petals; conical, tapering buds; narrow leaves

Buffalo Gourd

Sprawling stems; flowers with 5 large petals; fruit a green-striped ball; scratchy, ill-smelling leaves

Golden Columbine

Clumps to 4 feet tall; flowers have long, straight spurs; fan-shaped lobed leaflets

Allium cernuum

Nodding Onion

Nodding clusters; pink to white, urn-shaped flowers; grass-like leaves smell like onions

Allium geyeri

Geyer's Onion

Erect clusters; pink to white, urn-shaped flowers; grass-like leaves smell like onions

Allium macropetalum

Large-petaled Wild Onion

Erect clusters; urn-shaped, pink to white flowers, midstripe red; grass-like leaves smell like onions

Portulaca pilosa

Shaggy Portulaca

Sprawling stems have tufts of hair around flowers with 5 oval petals; tubular, succulent leaves

Allionia incarnata

Trailing Windmills

Prostrate stems 1–3 feet; 3 fan-shaped rose-to-magenta petals; oblong, sticky leaves

Potentilla thurberi

Red Cinquefoil

Stems 1–2 feet; 5 petals overlap, showy stamens; 5–7 leaflets radiate from stem

Asclepias speciosa

Showy Milkweed

Up to 4 feet tall; clusters of rose-pink flowers; seed pods covered with warty prickles; milky sap

Krameria lanceolata

Trailing Krameria

Hairy, sprawling stems, 8–40 inches; flowers have 4–5 wine-red sepals; linear, pointed leaves

Castilleja chromosa

Desert Paintbrush

Lobed, red-tipped bracts; yellowish, conical flowers; upper leaves have pointed lobes

Castilleja integra

Wholeleaf Paintbrush

Hairy stems, 4–20 inches; showy, red, unlobed bracts; unlobed leaves are hairy on bottoms only

Castilleja lanata

Woolly Paintbrush

Felt-like woolly stems, 4–36 inches; spikes have hairy red bracts; narrow, 3-lobed leaves

Castilleja linariifolia

Wyoming Paintbrush

Stems to 3 feet; red, lobed bracts; greenish, beak-like flowers; linear leaves are rolled inward

Castilleja miniata

Scarlet Paintbrush

Showy, fork-lobed red bracts surround small, yellowish, beak-shaped flowers; unlobed leaves

Chamerion angustifolium

Fireweed

Leafy, chest-high stems; spikes of pink flowers, 4 petals; forms dense stands on mountain slopes

Peritoma serrulata

Rocky Mountain Bee Plant

Stems 2–5 feet; dense flower clusters; 4 pink petals, long stamens; pods dangle; narrow leaflets

Zeltnera arizonica

Arizona Mountain Pink

Branching stems 8–16 inches; pink flowers with white throat; lance-shaped leaves; wet soils

Houstonia rubra

Red Bluet

Stems to 4 inches; trumpet-shaped, pink-to-white flowers; erect, needle-like leaves

Monarda citriodora

Lemon Beebalm

Stems 1–2 feet; pinkish flowers in dense whorls, pale to rose-purple bracts; lance-shaped leaves

Oenothera curtiflora

Velvet-leaf Gaura

Stems 2–7 feet; arching spikes have tiny pink-to-white flowers; oval leaves covered with soft hairs

Oenothera suffrutescens

Scarlet Gaura

Stems hairy, 8–20 inches; white flowers open at night, turn red next day; erect, cylindrical buds

Penstemon parryi

Parry's Penstemon

Stems to 4 feet; flowers have equal-sized lobes; clusters grow on opposite sides of stem; AZ

Penstemon eatonii

Firecracker Penstemon

2-foot stems; tubular flowers on one side of stem have small, rounded, equal-sized lobes

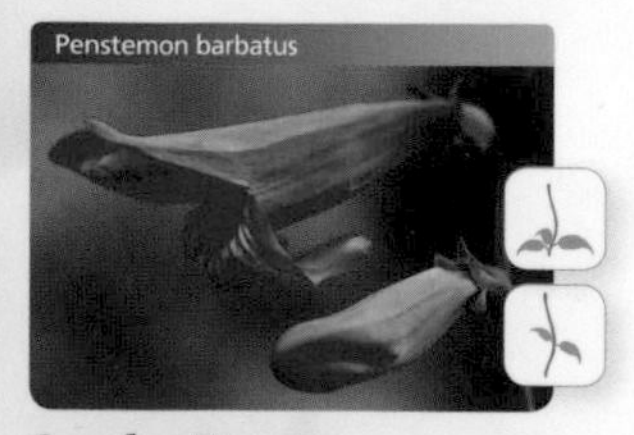
Penstemon barbatus

Scarlet Penstemon

Stems 12–40 inches; tubular flowers on one side of stem have lower lobes bent backwards

Penstemon palmeri

Palmer's Penstemon

Stems to 6 feet; inflated pink-to-white flowers grow in dense one-sided clusters; plant has thick, triangular leaves

Red to Pink

Lythrum californicum

California Loosestrife

Branching stems to 2 feet; tubular rose-purple flowers, throat white; linear to lance-shaped leaves

Ipomopsis aggregata

Skyrocket

Stems to 3 feet; red, trumpet-like flowers; spreading petals with white spots; threadlike leaves

Lonicera arizonica

Arizona Honeysuckle

Woody vine to 6 feet long; clusters of tubular flowers with 5 lobes; oval to elliptical leaves

Lobelia cardinalis

Cardinal Flower

Stems 2–6 feet tall; trumpet-shaped flowers with 5 spreading lobes; lance-shaped leaves

Salvia henryi

Red Sage

Stems to 20 inches; paired tubular flowers have a lobed lower lip; rounded, lobed leaflets

Stachys coccinea

Scarlet Hedgenettle

Stems 1–3 feet; spike of whorled, tubular, 2-lipped flowers; toothed, oval, veiny leaves

Fouquieria splendens

Ocotillo

Wand-like thorny stems, 8–20 feet; tubular flowers in spike at tips; leaves present only after rains

Anisacanthus thurberi

Desert Honeysuckle

Shrub 3–6 feet; red-orange, tubular flowers with curled lobes; lance-shaped leaves

Bouvardia ternifolia

Firecracker Bush

Shrub to 4 feet; clusters of tubular flowers with short, pointed lobes; lance-shaped leaves; AZ

Epilobium canum

Hummingbird Trumpet

Low, shrubby to 2 feet; tubular flowers with lobed, spreading petals, protruding stamens

Ipomoea cristulata

Scarlet Morning Glory

Twining vine; trumpet-shaped, red-to-orange flowers; roundish leaves with 3–5 deep lobes

Justicia californica

Hummingbird Bush/Chuparosa

Bushy shrub to 6 feet; flower tube tipped with 2 long lips; leaves often drop by flowering; AZ

Aquilegia desertorum

Red Columbine

Stems to 2 feet tall; nodding red flowers have yellowish-tipped petals and long, straight red spurs

Cosmos parviflorus

Southwest Cosmos

Stems 2–3 feet; rays pink to white; yellow disk flowers; leaves divided into thread-like lobes

Convolvulus arvensis

Field Bindweed

Mat-forming vine spreads to 6 feet; pink to white flowers; arrow-shaped leaves; weedy

Silene laciniata

Cardinal Catchfly

Stems branching, 1–2-feet tall; tubular flowers with 5 deeply cut petals with pointed lobes

Carduus nutans

Musk Thistle

Spiny stems to 15 feet; flower heads nod, spiny base, florets pink-purple; spiny leaves; invasive

Cirsium arizonicum

Arizona Thistle

Woolly stems, 1–5 feet; red to purple florets in erect column; leaves have spine-tipped lobes

Cirsium ochrocentrum

Yellow-spine Thistle

Stems 1–3 feet; flowers pink to white, spines ½-inch long; spiny twisted leaf lobes

Cirsium neomexicana

New Mexico Thistle

Woolly stems 1–6 feet; woolly, spiny flower head; leaves have deep, spine-tipped lobes

Cirsium undulatum

Wavyleaf Thistle

Stems 2–8 feet; spiny bracts with a white ridge; rose-purple flowers; wavy-lobed, spiny leaves

Rosa woodsii

Woods Rose

Thorny shrub, 3–9 feet; 5 petals; showy yellow stamens; 5–7 oval leaflets along midrib; forests

Gaillardia pulchella

Indian Blanket

Stems to 2 feet; rays with varying amounts of yellow and red; linear to spatula-shaped leaves

Calliandra eriophylla

Fairy Duster

Thornless shrub to 3 feet; spherical clusters with showy stamens; twice-compound leaves; AZ

White to Green

Chaenactis stevioides

Broad-flower Pincushion

Stems to 1 foot; spherical cluster of white-to-pinkish disk flowers; leaves have narrow lobes

Bistorta bistortoides

Western Bistort

Up to 2 feet; oblong cluster of tiny white-to-pink flowers; lance-shaped leaves; moist soils

Apocynum androsaemifolium

Spreading Dogbane

Erect, branching, to 3 feet tall; bell-shaped, slightly nodding flowers; broad, pointed leaves

Comandra umbellata

Bastard Toadflax

Stems 3–20 inches; creamy to pinkish petals, brown anthers; narrow to elliptic leaves; weedy

Anemopsis californica

Yerba Mansa

Up to 1 foot tall; spike with 4–9 white, petal-like lower bracts; smaller white bracts; wetlands

Abronia fragrans

Fragrant Sand Verbena

Stems 8–40 inches; snowball-like clusters of white, tubular flowers; oval, pointed leaves

Polygala alba

Milkwort

Stems 6–16 inches; spike of flowers with 3 united petals, 2 side wings; narrow, linear leaves

Achillea millefolium

Common Yarrow

Stems 1–3 feet tall; flat clusters of tiny, white flowers; fernlike, aromatic leaves

Cicuta maculata

Spotted Water Hemlock

Purple-spotted 2–9 foot stems; clusters of small flowers; lance-shaped leaflets; **deadly toxic**

Conium maculatum

Poison Hemlock

Purple-spotted stems to 10 feet; rounded flower clusters; parsley-like leaves; wet soils; **deadly toxic**

Heracleum maximum

Cow Parsnip

Stems to 8 feet; umbrella-shaped clusters of small, white flowers; large rounded, lobed leaves

Dalea candida

White Prairie-Clover

Clumping stems 2 feet tall; dense spikes; tiny flowers with yellow anthers; oblong to linear leaflets

Daucus pusillus

Wild Carrot

Stems 1–3 feet; spoked array tipped with clusters of small flowers; parsley-like leaflets

Lepidium montanum

Western Peppergrass

Clumps 6–20 inches; cylindrical spike; 4 petals on flowers; flat, round seeds; linear, lobed leaves

Dimorphocarpa wislizeni

Spectacle Pod Mustard

Stems to 2 feet; flowers in a dense cluster; fused twin, flat pods along stem; hairy, lobed leaves

Eriogonum jamesii

James Buckwheat

Stems to 10 inches; leaf-like bracts below clusters of hairy, creamy flowers; elliptic leaves

Wright's Buckwheat

Bushy clumps to 40 inches; white to pink flowers; elliptic, woolly leaves in bundles

Wild Candytuft

Stems to 1 foot; dense, rounded to elongated cluster; single, flat oval pods; clasping oval leaves

False Lily of the Valley

Stems 12–36 inches; plume of tiny feathery flowers; sword-like leaves with distinct parallel veins

Star Solomon's Seal

Stems 12–28 inches; clusters have one star-shaped flower per tiny branch; sword-like leaves

Mountain Death Camas

Flower spike 4–20 inches tall; creamy petals with V-shaped green spot; grass-like leaves

Antelope Horns Milkweed

Clumps 1–3 feet; spherical flower clusters; conical pods, fluffy seeds; narrow leaves; milky sap

Broadleaf Milkweed

Stems 2–3 feet; creamy-green clusters in leaf axils; thick, broad, dark green leaves; milky sap

Horsetail Milkweed

Stems 8–40 inches; creamy-to-white flowers in rounded clusters; long, narrow leaves; milky sap

Lathyrus lanszwertii

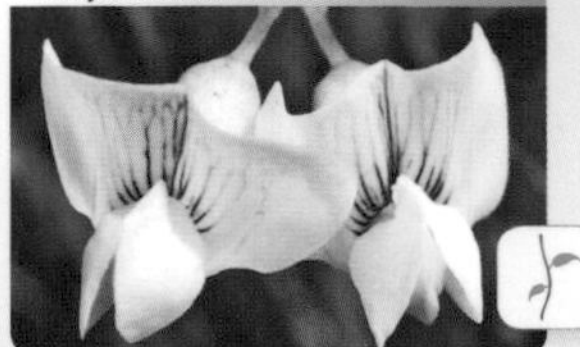

Nevada Peavine

Sprawling stems 4–16 inches; flower's upper banner petal has red lines; long, elliptic leaflets

Penstemon ambiguus

Bush Penstemon

Bushy to 3 feet; flower tube pink with white lobes; clusters grow around stem; narrow leaves

Aphanostephus ramosissimus

Plains Doze Daisy

Stems 4–20 inches; rays have red stripe below; yellow disk; linear to lobed leaves

Fragaria vesca

Wild Strawberry

Small white flowers and red berries; basal leaves have 3 leaflets with coarse teeth

Delphinium parishii

Desert Larkspur

Stems 1–2 feet; white, pink, or blue hairy flowers with tiny spurs; deeply lobed leaves; AZ

Nicotiana obtusifolia

Desert Tobacco

Leafy stem 7–26 inches; tubular, white, creamy, or greenish flowers; sticky, hairy leaves

Chaetopappa ericoides

Baby Aster

Stems 2–7 inches; rays fade to pink, tips curl; narrow leaves overlapping against stem

Monarda pectinata

Plains Beebalm

Hairy stems to 20 inches; whorled clusters with green bracts; leaves oblong to lance-shaped

White to Green

Polanisia dodecandra

Clammyweed

Stems to 2 feet; dense clusters of flowers with long purple stamens; sticky, fetid leaflets

Clematis ligusticifolia

Western Virgin's Bower

Vine; 4–5 hairy petals, showy stamens; fruit a silky plume; 5–15 lance-shaped leaflets; forests

Clematis drummondii

Old Man's Beard

Sprawling vine; flowers creamy, no petals; seeds a mass of feathery plumes; lobed leaflets

Zinnia acerosa

Dwarf Zinnia

Clumps 4–18 inches tall; oblong rays; disk yellow, turning brown; narrow, crowded leaves

Viola canadensis

Canada White Violet

Stems 8–15 inches; 5 spreading petals with yellow, dark-lined throat; heart-shaped leaves

Convolvulus equitans

Texas Bindweed

Twining stems to 6 feet long; white-to-pink flower; leaves narrow, pointed rear lobes

Geranium richardsonii

Richardson's Geranium

Stems 8–32 inches; white-to-pink purple-veined petals; leaves have toothed lobes; forests

Frasera speciosa

Monument Plant

Clusters of speckled green flowers line a 2- to 6-foot-tall stalk; stalks from a dense rosette of leaves

Melampodium leucanthum

Blackfoot Daisy

Stems 6–16 inches; narrow, notched rays; yellow disk; hairy, linear to lance-shaped leaves

Erigeron concinnus

Navajo Fleabane

Stems hairy, to 20 inches; narrow, white-to-pinkish rays; yellow disk; thin hairy leaves

Erigeron divergens

Spreading Fleabane

Branching, hairy stems to 20 inches; white to purplish rays; yellow disk; narrow leaves

Symphyotrichum falcatum

White Prairie Aster

Stems 10–30 inches; daisy-like flowers, 20–35 rays, yellow-brown disk; short, narrow leaves

Calycoseris wrightii

White Tackstem

Stems 2–12 inches; petals have 5 points, yellow center; no disk florets; narrow, lobed leaves

Townsendia exscapa

Stemless Townsend Daisy

Stemless mats 2 inches high; 11–40 white rays, yellow disk with white bristles; narrow leaves

Calochortus gunnisonii

Gunnison's Mariposa Lily

Stems 10–20 inches; petals white with purple band and yellow hairs; narrow leaves

Calochortus nuttallii

Sego Lily

Stems 6–17 inches; white petals with maroon crescents and yellow base; narrow leaves

White to Green

Argemone pleiacantha

Southwest Prickly Poppy

Prickly stems 2–4 feet; flowers have 6 crinkly petals; yellow filaments; lobed, prickly leaves

Yucca baccata

Banana Yucca

Trunkless; flower cluster mostly within leaves; ridged sword-like leaves lined with shredding threads

Yucca baileyi

Navajo Yucca

Trunkless; dense flower cluster begins within leaves; narrow, flexible leaves lined with threads

Yucca brevifolia

Joshua Tree Yucca

Trunk to 45 feet tall tipped with dense clusters of flowers; dagger-like leaves, no threads; AZ

Yucca elata

Soaptree Yucca

Trunks to 15 feet plus; flower cluster on 3- to 7-foot stem; narrow, flexible leaves with threads

Oenothera albicaulis

Prairie Evening Primrose

Sprawling stems 1–2 feet; 4 heart-shaped petals, buds nod; wavy to lobed, hairy leaves

Oenothera caespitosa

Tufted Evening Primrose

Stemless; flower tube to 6 inches long; notched petals, erect buds; hairy, elliptical, lobed leaves

Datura wrightii

Sacred Datura

Sprawling stems 3–4 feet; trumpet-shaped flowers; spiny fruit; oval to triangular leaves

Blue to Magenta

Abronia angustifolia

Purple Sand-Verbena

Stems to 20 inches; spherical cluster of pink to magenta, tubular flowers; oval, pointed leaves

Glandularia bipinnatifida

Prairie Verbena

Sprawling stems 4–24 inches; rounded clusters of purple-to-pink flowers; lobed leaves

Nama hispida

Purplemat

Low-mounding, 4–20 inches; lavender to purple, yellow throat; hairy leaves, edges rolled under

Agastache pallidiflora

Giant Hyssop

Stems 1–4 feet; spikes have purple, rose, or white, tubular flowers; triangular, toothed leaves

Eriastrum diffusum

Miniature Woolly Star

Stems to 12 inches; purple-to-white flowers, yellow-to-white throats; narrow, lobed leaves

Delphinium nuttallianum

Dwarf Larkspur

Stems 4–16 inches; spike; petals form tube with spur; round, deeply lobed leaves; dry sites

Delphinium scaposum

Barestem Larkspur

Leafless stems 8–20 inches; spike has 5–15 blue flowers with white inner petals; lobed leaves

Dalea formosa

Feather Dalea

Low-mounding shrub 2–3 feet; flowers violet with a yellow lobe, hairy plumes; tiny, oblong leaflets

Woolly Prairie-Clover

Sprawling, woolly stems 1–2 feet; cylindrical flower spike; leaves have 5–17 woolly leaflets

Many-flowered Ipomopsis

Stems 6–16 inches; clusters of trumpet-shaped flowers with purple dots; narrow leaves

Sawtooth Sage

Stems to 18 inches; spike has whorled flowers, white-spotted lower lip; toothed leaves

Nuttall's Milkvetch

Stems to 18 inches; lilac-and-white flowers; flat, curved pods; leaves have 7–19 small leaflets

Freckled Milkvetch

Clumps to 3 feet wide; tubular purple-and-white flowers; freckled, inflated pods; 7–25 leaflets

Woolly Locoweed

Stems 2 inches long with dense cluster of white-woolly leaves; tubular flowers; oval, woolly pods

Gay Feather

Stems 1–3 feet; plume-like spikes dense with lavender florets; narrow, linear leaves

Snapdragon Vine

Low-climbing vine; small, tubular flowers with spreading lobes, white throat; triangular leaves

Lupinus brevicaulis

Short-stem Lupine

Hairy 2- to 4-inch flower stems; rounded clusters; long-stemmed leaves have 5–8 hairy leaflets

Lupinus concinnus

Bajada Lupine

Stems 2–12 inches; spike often shorter than leaves; densely hairy leaves have 5–8 leaflets

Lupinus sparsiflorus

Arroyo Lupine

Hairy, 8- to 16-inch stems; flowers in 6– to 8-inch spikes; leaves have 7–11 radiating, hairy leaflets

Lupinus argenteus

Silvery Lupine

Up to 4 feet; silvery-hairy flowers with a swollen, pointed base; 5–10 radiating leaflets

Oxytropis lambertii

Purple Locoweed

Plant silky-hairy; flower stems to 12 inches; cylindrical pods; leaves have 7–19 linear leaflets

Mertensia franciscana

Franciscan Bluebells

Leafy stems 2–3 feet; funnel-shaped, hanging flowers; elliptic, veined leaves; moist areas

Nuttallanthus texanus

Texas Toadflax

Stems to 30 inches; light-blue-to-whitish flowers, down-curved rear spur; linear to oval leaves

Campanula rotundifolia

Harebell

Stems 4–24 inches; bell-shaped, nodding flowers; 5 petals, pointed, spreading; narrow leaves

Purple Aster

Flower clusters on 2-foot stems; heads crowded with slender, blue-to-purple rays, yellow disk

Blue Flax

Flowers with 5 delicate petals last only one day; narrow, pointed leaves hug the stem

Narrow-leaf Four O'Clock

Stems to 3 feet; pink-purple-to-white flowers, 5 notched petals; narrow leaves

Stork's Bill

Sprawling stems to 18 inches long; round-tipped, purple-to-lavender petals; deeply cut leaves

Spiny Bluebowls

Stems 3–6 inches; dark blue petals, yellow throat, yellow anthers; needle-like, lobed leaves

Venus Looking Glass

Stems 4–36 inches; flowers have a white throat; roundish leaves clasp stem; milky sap

Violet Wood Sorrel

Flower stems 4–10 inches; 5 petals with whitish throats; leaves have 3 heart-shaped leaflets

Purple Groundcherry

Mat-forming stems 4–6 inches high; crinkly petals, yellow anthers; berry in a lantern-like sack

Hooked-spur Violet

Blue-to-violet flowers; whitish throats have dark lines; oval to triangular basal leaves

Toadflax Beardtongue

Slender, bell-shaped, pale-blue-to-violet flowers grow singly on one side of stem; narrow leaves

Fendler's Penstemon

Slender, tubular, lavender-to-purple flowers in clusters around stem; leaves fold along midvein

Rocky Mountain Penstemon

Stems 8–27 inches; tubular, blue-purple flowers on one side of spike; narrow, pointed leaves

Dusky Penstemon

Inflated tubular, maroon-to-blue flowers; clusters on one side of stem; lance-shaped leaves

Pale Trumpets

Stems 4–24 inches; long, tubular, blue-to-whitish flowers; narrow, linear leaves

Owl Clover

Clumps to 16 inches tall; flower spikes have showy crimson bracts; hairy, lobed leaves; AZ

Wild Bergamot

Stems 12–30 inches; spherical flower head of purple-to-pink, tubular flowers; leaves are oval or lance-shaped

Gentiana affinis

Pleated Gentian

Stems 20–40 inches; tubular, clustered flowers barely open; oblong leaves; mountain meadows

Geranium caespitosum

Purple Geranium

Stems 8–28 inches; purple-to-pink petals, showy stamen column; fan-shaped, deeply cut leaves

Machaeranthera tanacetifolia

Tansy Daisy

Clumping stems to 1 foot; purple-to-violet flower rays, yellow disk; fern-like, spine-tipped leaves

Solanum elaeagnifolium

Silver-leaf Nightshade

Prickly stems 1–3 feet; wrinkled petals; yellow, toxic berries; narrow to oblong silvery-hairy leaves

Commelina dianthifolia

Birdbill Dayflower

Stems to 10 inches; flowers bloom from boat-like sack; long, narrow leaves sheathe stem

Tradescantia occidentalis

Western Spiderwort

Fleshy stems to 20 inches; 3 oval blue-to-rose petals; narrow, blade-like leaves sheathe stem

Cordylanthus wrightii

Wright's Bird's Beak

Stems to 20 inches; cluster of tubular, lavender-to-yellow flowers; threadlike leaves

Aconitum columbianum

Columbian Monkshood

Stems 1–6 feet; flowers with hood-like upper petals; leaves deeply lobed; **all parts toxic**

Blue to Magenta

Aquilegia coerulea

Blue Columbine

Stems 1–3 feet; blue-and-white flowers have spreading petals and long spurs; 3-lobed leaves

Clematis hirsutissima

Hairy Leatherflower

Stems 6–24 inches; nodding, hairy, urn-shaped flower, tips spreading; 7–13 narrow leaflets

Clematis columbiana

Rocky Mountain Clematis

Viny stems; bell-shaped, nodding pale-to-dark-blue flowers; deeply lobed leaves, 3 lobes

Mirabilis multiflora

Giant Four O'Clock

Mounding groundcover to 4 feet in diameter; bell-shaped flowers; thick, heart-shaped leaves

Erigeron speciosus

Showy Fleabane

Leafy stems to 30 inches; lavender-to-white rays; yellow disk; lance-shaped, hairless leaves

Calochortus flexuosus

Winding Mariposa Lily

Stems sprawl to 16 inches; lavender petals with yellow-and-orange spotted base

Iris missouriensis

Wild Iris

Stems 8–24 inches; blue, veined petals, white-and-yellow throat; broad, linear leaves

Proboscidea parviflora

Devil's Claw

Mounding stems 4–6 feet wide; tubular flowers have magenta, pink, or white lobes; hooked pods

Cacti

Opuntia engelmannii

Engelmann's Prickly Pear

Shrubby to 4 feet high with oval pads; uniformly yellow petals; barrel-shaped purple fruit

Opuntia polyacantha

Plains Prickly Pear

Sprawling clumps, 1–2 pads high; wrinkled pads, 3–5 inches; yellow petals; tan, dry fruit

Opuntia macrorhiza

Grassland Prickly Pear

Sprawling clumps, 1–2 pads high; pads wrinkled, 3–5 inches; yellow petals, red base; red fruit

Opuntia phaeacantha

Brown-spine Prickly Pear

Clumps 1–2 feet high; oval pads 4–13 inches long; yellow petals, red base; red fruit

Opuntia macrocentra

Purple Prickly Pear

Clumps to 3 feet high; green pads, purple if stressed; yellow petals, red base; red fruit

Opuntia basilaris

Beaver-tail Prickly Pear

Clumps to 15 inches high; pads usually spineless but with barbed bristles; tan fruit; AZ

Cylindropuntia leptocaulis

Christmas Cactus

Jointed thorny, bushy stems to 5 feet; pale yellow flower; red, fleshy, cylindrical fruit

Cylindropuntia bigelovii

Teddy Bear Cholla

Shrubby and covered with straw-colored spines; pale-green flowers, green filaments, and orange anthers

Cacti

Cylindropuntia imbricata

Cane Cholla

Cylindrical stems 3- to 9-feet tall have wicked spines and barbed bristles; pink-to-magenta flowers

Ferocactus cylindraceus

California Barrel

Cylindrical stems to 5 feet tall, 16 inches wide; flowers circle tip; flat, curved central spines; AZ

Echinocereus coccineus

Claret Cup

Ribbed, cylindrical, clumping stems to 8 inches tall; firm, spoon-shaped, waxy-looking petals

Echinocereus fendleri

Pink-flowering Hedgehog

Rippled, single or clumping, cylindrical stems to 7 inches; 1 long central spine curves upward

Sclerocactus parviflorus

Small-flower Fishhook

Ribbed single or clumped stems to 10 inches; flowers at stem apex; hooked lower central spine

Mammillaria grahamii

Graham's Nipple Cactus

Cylindrical stems 6 inches lined with nipples; flowers circle stem below tip; hooked central spine

Coryphantha vivipara

Beehive

Cylindrical stems to 8 inches, lined with nipples; flowers have slender, pointed petals at stem tip

Carnegiea gigantea

Saguaro

Single-ribbed, spine-lined trunk with arm-like branches; tubular flowers; iconic Arizona cactus

Adventure Quick Guides

Only Arizona & New Mexico Wildflowers

Organized by color for quick and easy identification

Simple and convenient—narrow your choices by color and leaf attachment, and view just a few wildflowers at a time

- Pocket-size format—easier than laminated foldouts
- Professional photos of flowers in bloom
- Similar colors grouped together to ensure that you quickly find what you're looking for
- Leaf icons for comparison and identification
- Easy-to-use information for even casual observers
- Expert author who is a longtime botanist and a skilled nature photographer

Get these *Adventure Quick Guides* for your area

ISBN 978-1-59193-817-0 $9.95

Adventure Publications
an imprint of AdventureKEEN
NATURE/WILDFLOWERS/SOUTHWEST